Getting Ready 2 Handwriting

First Edition

Copyright 2016 Lee Giles
All Rights Reserved
ISBN-13: 978-1530559763
ISBN-10: 1530559766

Day 1

This is the only day without a writing lesson for you to do, so I'll use today to give you some directions. You can use this book to do all of your handwriting for the year. The online directions may say something like, "Write a sentence from your lesson." When it does, I've included a sentence in this book ready for you to copy. It will make it so you don't have to be online in order to do your writing.

Now you can take this page to draw a picture of yourself writing. That's one of the big things you are going to learn this year. You are going to write words, write sentences, write your phone number, and more!

Day 2

Uppercase L

Write an L in each box. Start near the middle of the top of the box. Draw a line straight down to the bottom. Draw the line over to the right edge of the box. Circle your best one.

Day 3

Uppercase T

Write a T in each box. Start on the top middle of the box. Draw a line down to the bottom. Jump up to the top and draw a line from one corner to the other. We JUMP back up to the top instead of drawing another line back up because it's hard to draw right on top of your first line. Circle your best one.

Day 4

Uppercase I

Write an *I* in each box. Start on the top middle of the box. Draw a line to the bottom of the box. Jump back up to the top. Draw a line across the top of the box. Then jump to the bottom and draw a line across the bottom of the box. Circle your best one.

Day 5

Uppercase F

Write an F in each box. Start in the top corner of the box. Draw a line to the bottom of the box. Jump back up to the top of the box. Draw a line across the top of the box. Jump down to the middle of the box. Draw a line from one side of the box to almost the whole way across the box. Circle your best one.

Day 6

Uppercase E

Write an E in each box. E is just like F but you have to jump down one more time to draw a line across the bottom. Circle your best one.

Color in the zero.

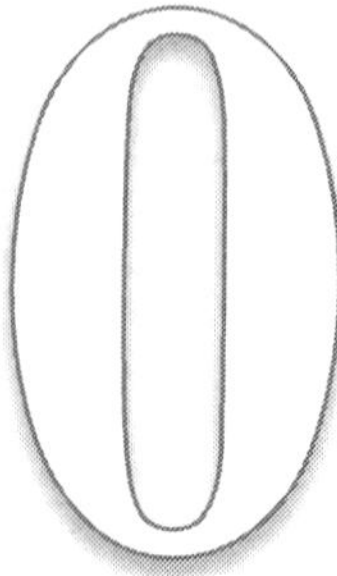

Day 7

Words

Count the number of boxes on the page. Touch each one and count it. There are ten. Now you are going to write three words in those ten boxes. You'll write one word on each line of boxes. Write: F E E L   I T   L I F T

Day 8

Uppercase H

Write an H in each box. Start in the top left corner and draw a line down the side of the box. Then jump up to the other corner and draw a line down. Then jump to the middle and draw a line across. Circle your best one.

<u>Day 9</u>

Uppercase M

Write an M in each box. Start in the top left corner, like you did with H. Draw a line down the side of the box. Then jump up to the corner and draw a diagonal line to the bottom middle of the box. (It'll be a little squashy.) Keep going back up to the top right corner. Draw a line down the side of the box to the bottom. Circle your best one.

Day 10

Uppercase N

Write an N in each box. Start in the top left corner. Draw a line down the side of the box to the bottom. Jump back up to the top and draw a line down to the opposite bottom corner. Then draw straight up to the top. Circle your best one.

Day 11

Uppercase V

Write a V in each box. Start in the top left corner. Draw down to the bottom middle and back up to the top right corner. Circle your best one.

Color in the one.

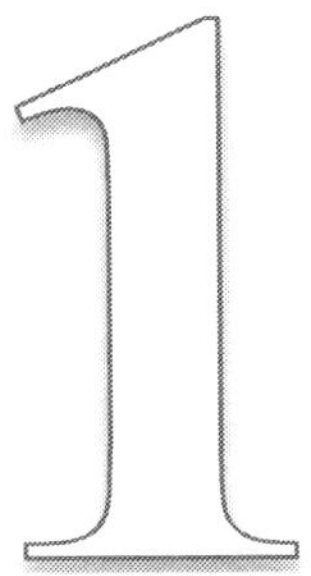

Day 12

Uppercase W

Write a W in each box. You write it like two Vs put together. Circle your best one.

Day 13

Words

Now you are going to write three words. You'll write one word on each line of boxes. Write: W I N H I M L I V E

Day 14

Uppercase X

Write an X in each box. Start in the top left corner and go down to the opposite corner at the bottom. Jump up to the top right corner and go down to the opposite bottom corner. Circle your best one.

Day 15

Uppercase Y

Write a Y in each box. Start in the top left and go down to the middle and back up to the top right. Jump to the bottom point of what you just wrote and draw straight down. Circle your best one.

<u>Day 16</u>

Uppercase K

Write a K in each box. Start at the top left corner. Draw a line down the side of the box. Jump up to the opposite corner at the top and draw a slanted line to the middle and then back out to the bottom corner. Circle your best one.

Day 17

Uppercase A

Write an A in each box. Start in the top middle. Draw a line down to the bottom left corner. Jump back up to the top and draw a line down to the bottom right corner. Jump up halfway and draw a line across the middle. Circle your best one.

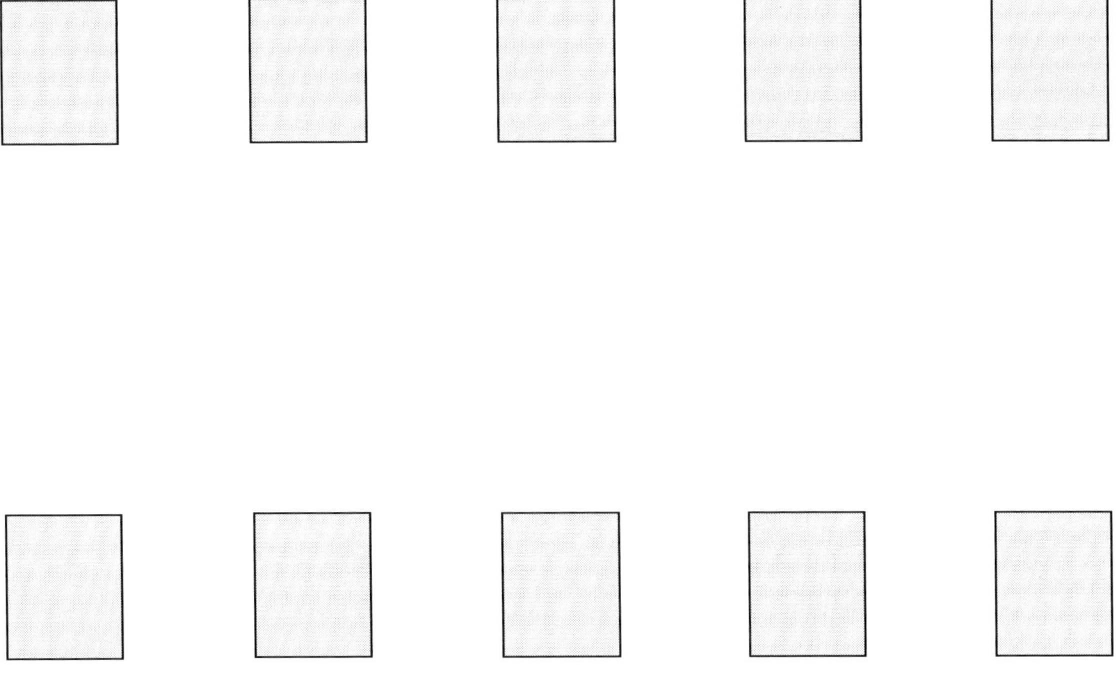

Color in the two.

2

Day 18

Uppercase Z

Write a Z in each box. Start in the top left and draw across the top of the box to the top right corner. Then draw down to the bottom left corner of the box and then across the bottom of the box to the other corner. Circle your best one.

Day 19

Words

Now you are going to write three words. You'll write one word on each line of boxes. Write: F I X   K A Y   K I T E

Day 20

Uppercase O and Q

Write an O in each box. Start at the top and draw a circle. Circle your best one. Then add a tail to each to turn them into Qs.

Day 21

Uppercase C

Write a C in each box. C is like part of an O. Circle your best one.

Color in the three.

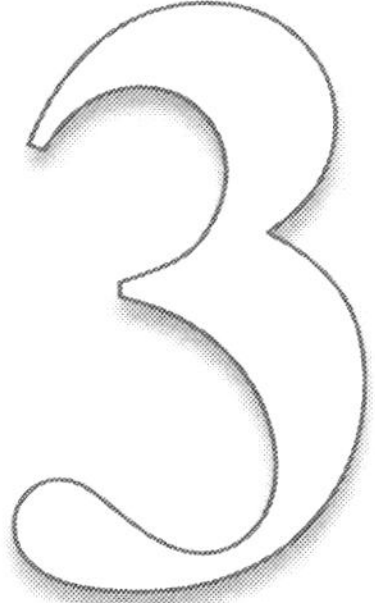

Day 22

Uppercase G

Write a G in each box. G is like a C with a little shelf drawn on top of the end. Circle your best one.

Color in the four.

Day 23

Uppercase U

Write a U in each box. Start in the top middle. Start at the top and curve down and back up. Make sure you touch the bottom of the box and go all the way back up to the top of the box. Circle your best one.

Color in the five.

5

Day 24

Uppercase J

Write a J in each box. Start in the top middle and draw down and then curve to the edge of the box. Draw a line across the top of the box. Circle your best one.

Day 25

Words

Now you are going to write three words. You'll write one word on each line of boxes. Write: J U G F O X C A K E

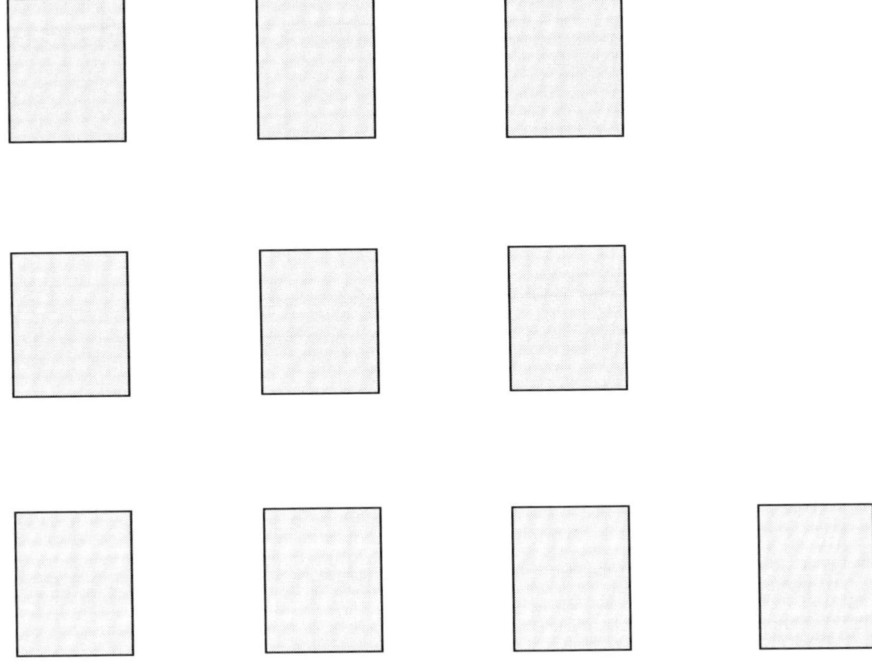

Color in the six.

6

Day 26

Uppercase S

Write an S in each box. Start on the top right of the box and curve your way down to the bottom left of the box. Make sure you touch the top and bottom of the box. Circle your best one.

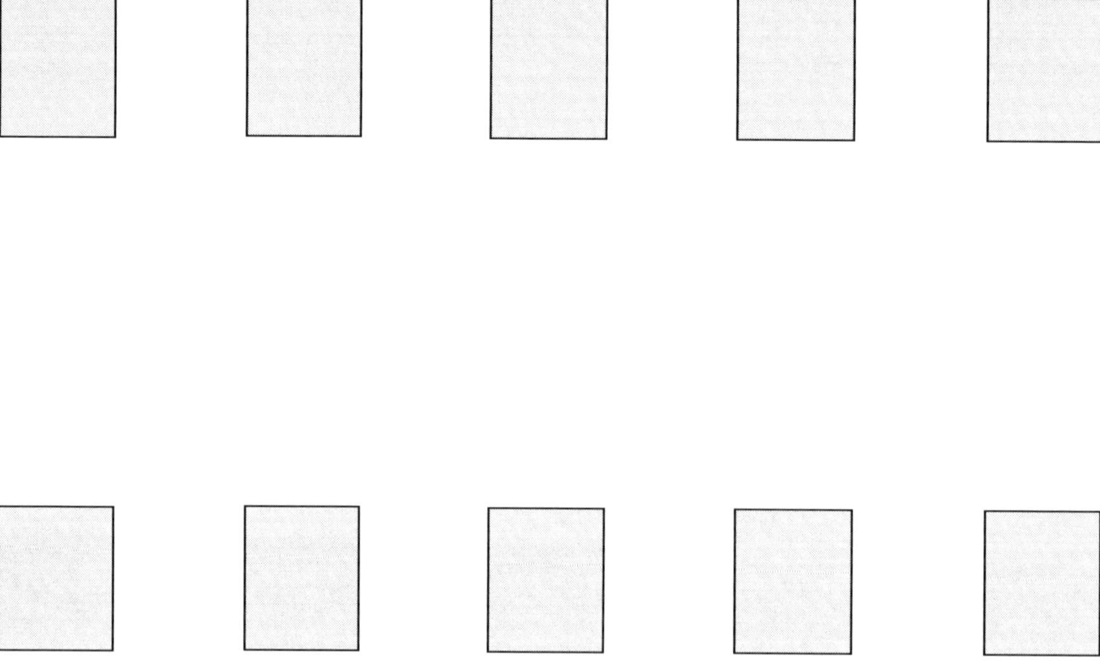

Color in the seven.

Day 27

Uppercase D

Write a D in each box. Start in the top left corner. Draw a line down the side of the box to the bottom of the box. Jump back up to the top. Draw a curve down to the bottom corner so that it meets your first line. Circle your best one.

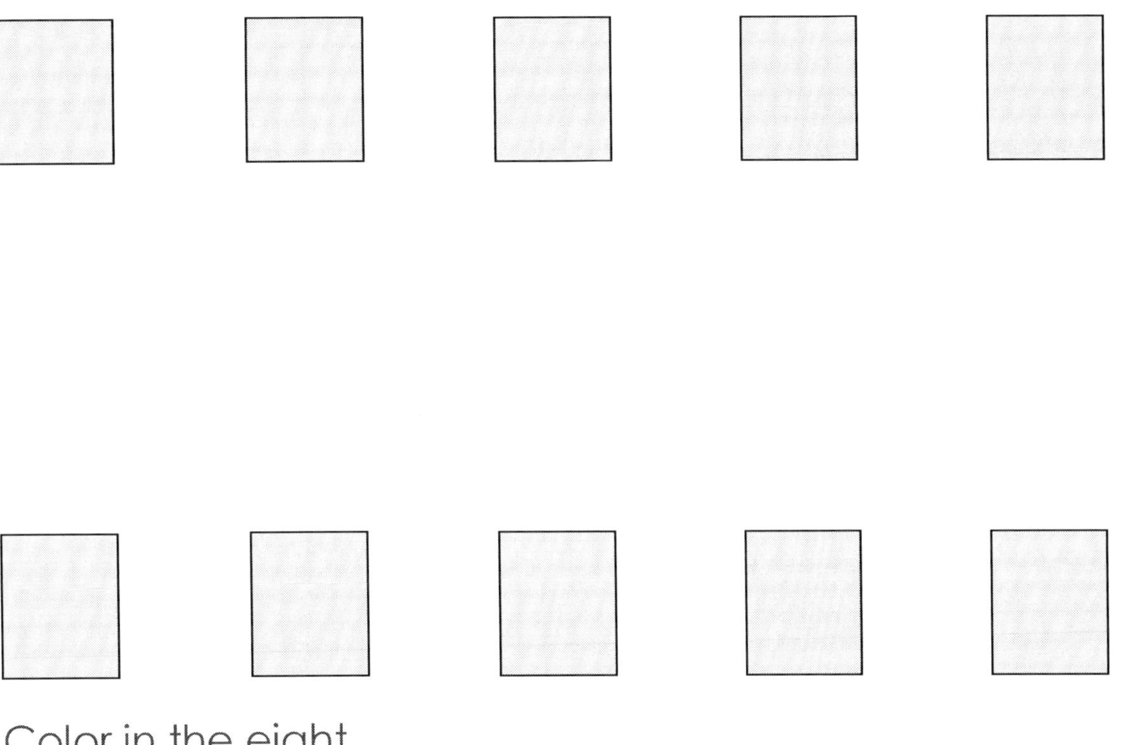

Color in the eight.

8

Day 28

Uppercase P

Write a P in each box. Start in the top left corner. Draw a line down the left side of the box. Jump back up to the top and draw a curve back to the middle of the line. Circle your best one.

Color in the nine.

9

Day 29

Uppercase R

Write an R in each box. Draw a P and then add a leg. Circle your best one.

Day 30

Uppercase B

Write a B in each box. Draw a P and then add a belly. Circle your best one.

Day 31

Words

Now you are going to write three words. You'll write one word on each line of boxes. Write: P A D S B R I C K S

Day 32

Your Name

Ask a parent or older sibling to write your name in the row of blocks. Now you write your name in the other rows. **Use all CAPS.**

Day 33

Lowercase C

In the block, write a big letter C. Next to it write a whole row of little c. On your sheet the block goes up high for the big, or capital C. When you write your little c, it will only go between the two lines on the paper. The top of the little c will touch the top line and the bottom of the little c will touch the bottom line. Circle your best one.

Day 34

Lowercase A

In the block on your page, write a big letter A. Next to it write a whole row of little a. It starts like a c, and then has one more line. Draw a little c and then jump to the top line and draw a side line down to make the a. Circle the best one.

Day 35

Lowercase D

In the block write a big letter D. Next to it write a whole row of little d. To write d you start by writing a little c, then you jump up above the top line and draw a line down. It's like an *a* but with an arm reaching up. Circle the best one.

<u>Day 36</u>

Writing Words

Write the words: add, cad, add. Put your finger down to make a space between each word.

Day 37

Lowercase G

In the block on your page, write a big letter G. Next to it write a whole row of little g. To write a g, you will start with writing a little c. You then close the c like you are writing an a, *but* you keep going and give it a tail. Circle your best one.

Day 38

Lowercase O

In the block on your page, write a big letter O. Next to it write a whole row of little o. Circle your best one.

Day 39

Lowercase B

In the block on your page, write a big letter B. Next to it write a whole row of little b. The letter b has an arm that reaches up over the top line. Circle your best one.

Day 40

Writing Words

Write the words: bog, bad, good. Put your finger down to make a space between each word.

<u>Day 41</u>

Lowercase P

In the block on your page, write a big letter P. Next to it write a whole row of little p. Little p is one of the letters with a tail that goes down below the line. Circle your best one.

Day 42

Lowercase Q

In the block on your page, write a big letter Q. Next to it write a whole row of little q. Little q is one of the letters with a tail that goes down below the line. Circle your best one.

Day 43

Lowercase E

In the block on your page, write a big letter E. Next to it write a whole row of little e. Little e starts in the middle and circles up to touch the top line and down to touch the bottom line. If you are unsure, ask someone to show you how to write it. Circle your best one.

Day 44

Writing Words

Write the words: peg, bed, goop. Put your finger down to make a space between each word.

Day 45

Lowercase L

In the block on your page, write a big letter L. Next to it write a whole row of little l. Little l is one of the letters that reaches up above the top line. Circle your best one.

Day 46

Lowercase T

In the block on your page, write a big letter T. Next to it write a whole row of little t. Little t is another one of the letters that reaches up above the top line. Circle your best one.

Day 47

Lowercase H

In the block on your page, write a big letter H. Next to it write a whole row of little h. Little h is one of the letters that reaches up above the line. Circle your best one.

Day 48

Writing Words

Write the words: hat, hot, bell. Put your finger down to make a space between each word.

Day 49

Lowercase K

In the block on your page, write a big letter K. Next to it write a whole row of little k. Little k is one of the letters that reaches up above the line. Circle your best one.

k

Day 50

Lowercase I

In the block on your page, write a big letter I. Next to it write a whole row of little i. To write little i you start on the top line and draw straight down. Then you jump up and put the dot above the line. Circle your best one.

Day 51

Lowercase J

In the block on your page, write a big letter J. Next to it write a whole row of little j. Little j is one of the letters that has a tail under the bottom line. Circle your best one.

Day 52

Writing Words

Write the words: jig, kid, kite. Put your finger down to make a space between each word.

Day 53

Lowercase F

In the block on your page, write a big letter F. Next to it write a whole row of little f. Little f is one of the letters that reaches up above the line. Circle your best one.

Day 54

Lowercase N

In the block on your page, write a big letter N. Next to it write a whole row of little n. Circle your best one.

Day 55

Lowercase M

In the block on your page, write a big letter M. Next to it write a whole row of little m. Little m starts like n but has an extra bump. Circle your best one.

<u>Day 56</u>

Writing Words

Write the words: flap, men, ninja. Put your finger down to make a space between each word.

Day 57

Lowercase R

In the block on your page, write a big letter R. Next to it write a whole row of little r. Circle your best one.

Day 58

Lowercase S

In the block on your page, write a big letter S. Next to it write a whole row of little s. Circle your best one.

s

Day 59

Lowercase U

In the block on your page, write a big letter U. Next to it write a whole row of little u. Circle your best one.

Day 60

Writing Words

Write the words: runs, slurp, turn. Put your finger down to make a space between each word.

Day 61

Lowercase V

In the block on your page, write a big letter V. Next to it write a whole row of little v. Circle your best one.

Day 62

Lowercase W

In the block on your page, write a big letter W. Next to it write a whole row of little w. Little w stays between the lines. Circle your best one.

w

Day 63

Lowercase Y

In the block on your page, write a big letter Y. Next to it write a whole row of little y. Little y has a tail that hangs down below the line. Circle your best one.

Day 64

Writing Words

Write the words: wavy, valley, win. Put your finger down to make a space between each word.

<u>Day 65</u>

Lowercase X

In the block on your page, write a big letter X. Next to it write a whole row of little x. Little x stays between the lines. Circle your best one.

x

Day 66

Lowercase Z

In the block on your page, write a big letter Z. Next to it write a whole row of little z. Little z stays between the lines. Circle your best one.

Day 67

Writing Words

Write the words: zoo, box, zebra. Put your finger down to make a space between each word.

Day 68

Writing

Write your first name. The first letter should be a big letter. The other letters should be little, lowercase letters.

Day 69

Practice

Trace the letter. Then fill the row with your own. Then write the matching uppercase letter in the block.

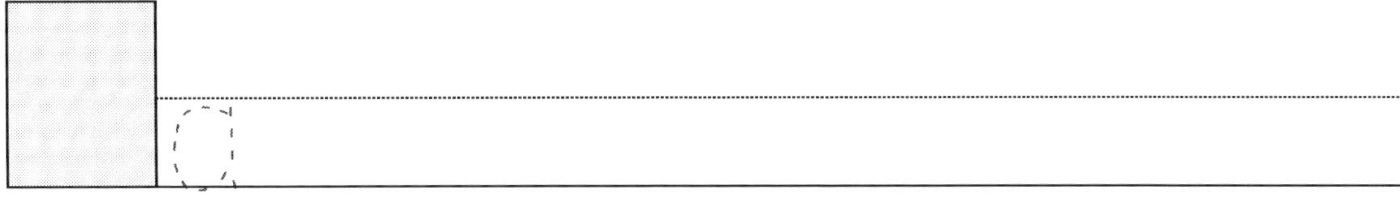

Day 70

Practice

Trace the letter. Then fill the row with your own. Then write the matching uppercase letter in the block.

Day 71

Practice

Trace the letter. Then fill the row with your own. Then write the matching uppercase letter in the block.

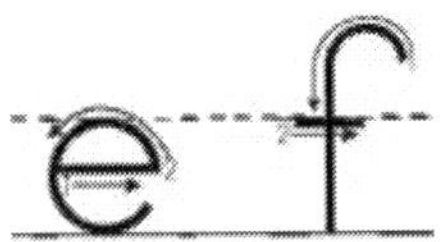

Day 72

Practice

Trace the letter. Then fill the row with your own. Then write the matching uppercase letter in the block.

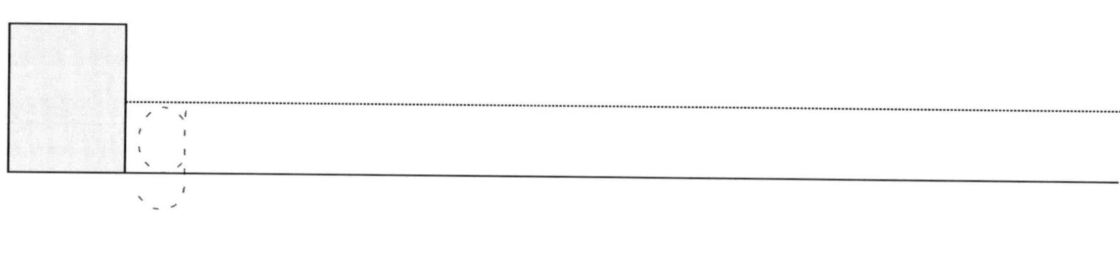

Day 73

Practice

Trace the letter. Then fill the row with your own. Then write the matching uppercase letter in the block.

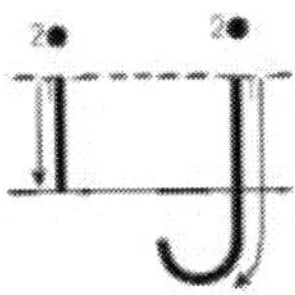

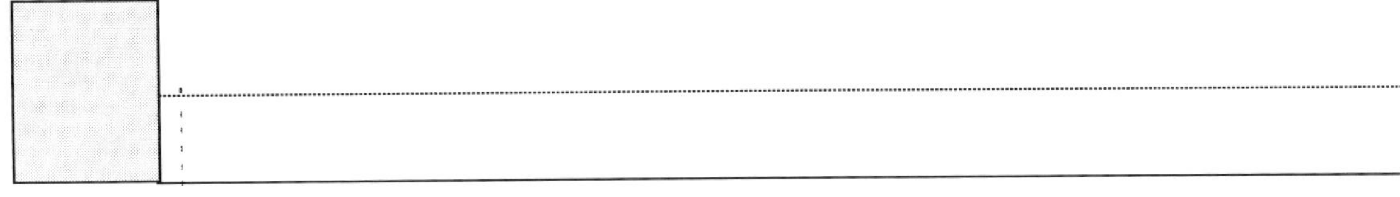

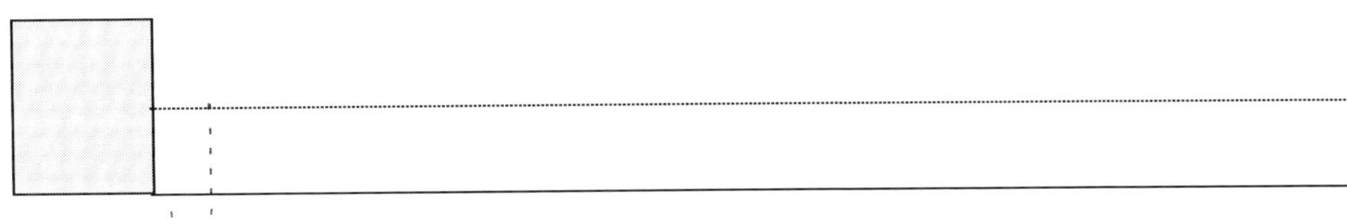

Day 74

Practice

Trace the letter. Then fill the row with your own. Then write the matching uppercase letter in the block.

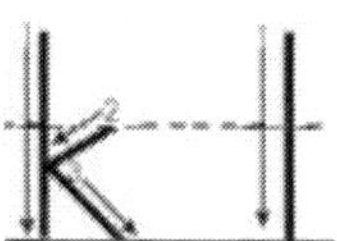

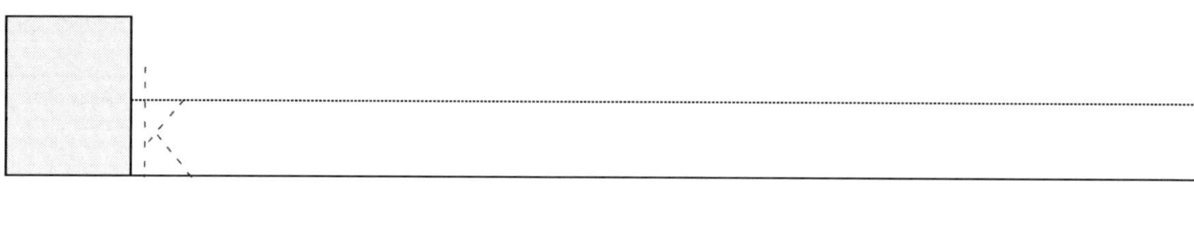

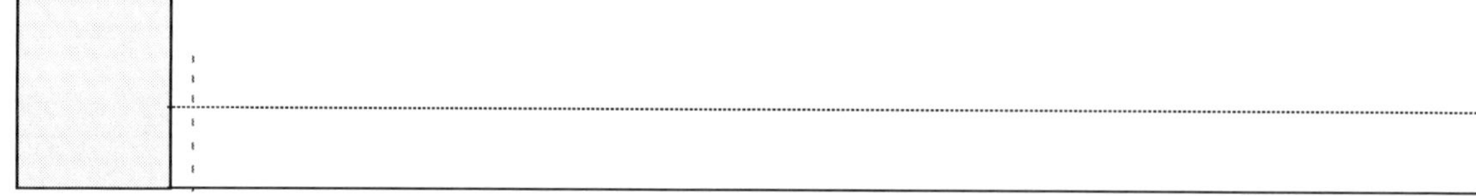

Day 75

Practice

Trace the letter. Then fill the row with your own. Then write the matching uppercase letter in the block.

m n

Day 76

Practice

Trace the letter. Then fill the row with your own. Then write the matching uppercase letter in the block.

o p

Day 77

Practice

Trace the letter. Then fill the row with your own. Then write the matching uppercase letter in the block.

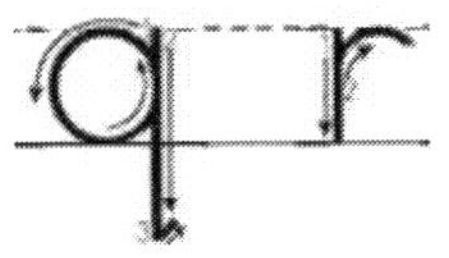

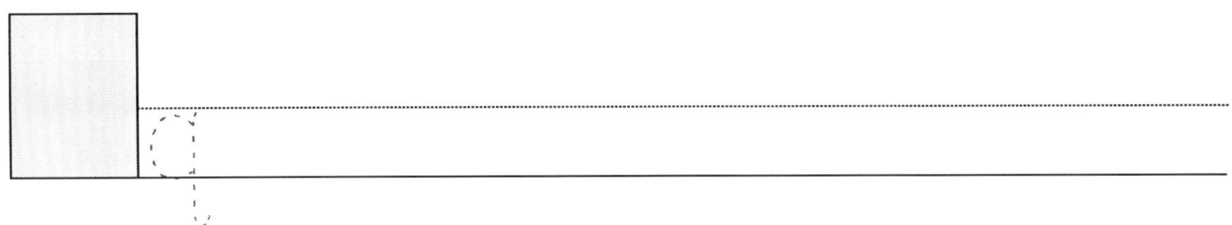

Day 78

Practice

Trace the letter. Then fill the row with your own. Then write the matching uppercase letter in the block.

Day 79

Practice

Trace the letter. Then fill the row with your own. Then write the matching uppercase letter in the block.

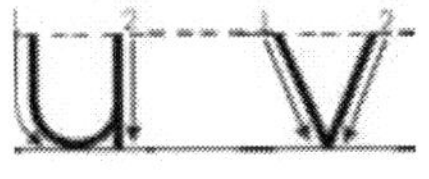

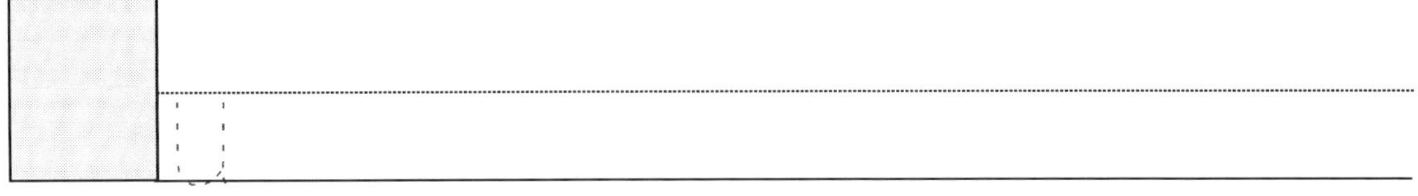

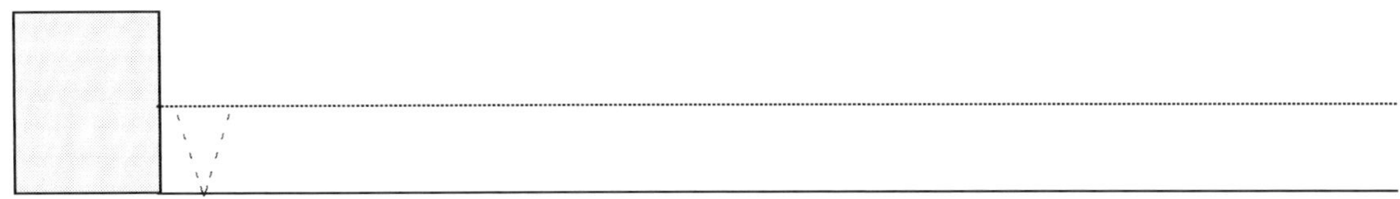

Day 80

Practice

Trace the letter. Then fill the row with your own. Then write the matching uppercase letter in the block.

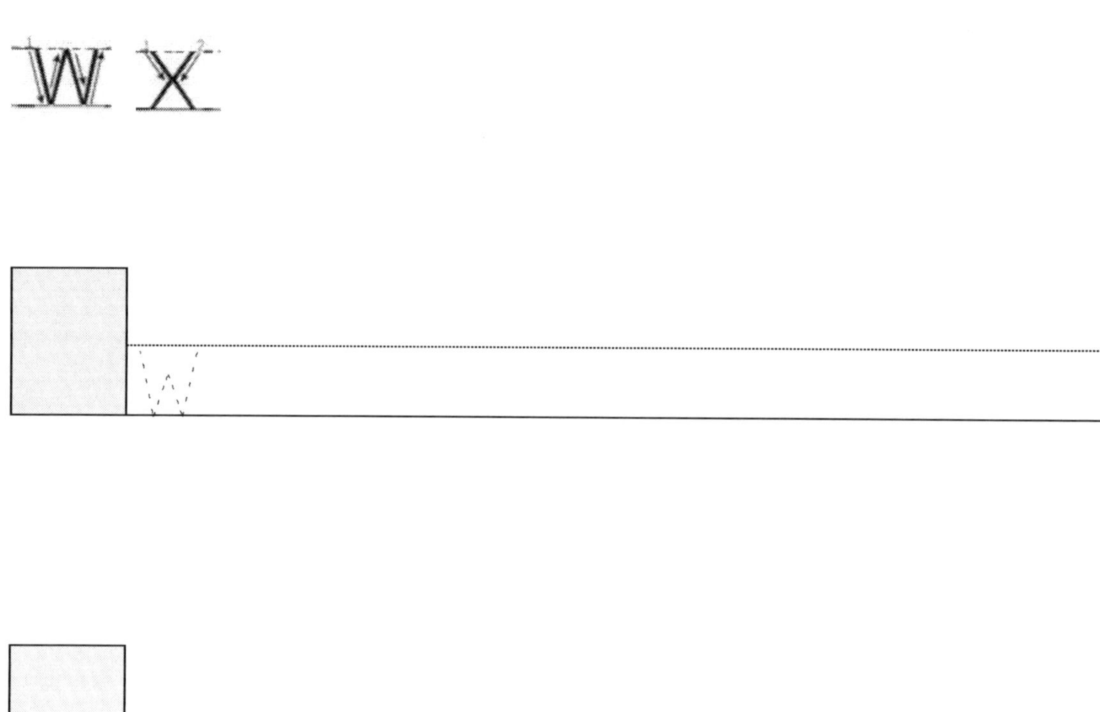

Day 81

Practice

Trace the letter. Then fill the row with your own. Then write the matching uppercase letter in the block.

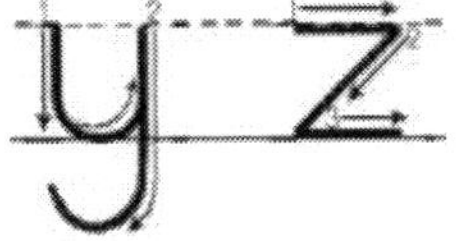

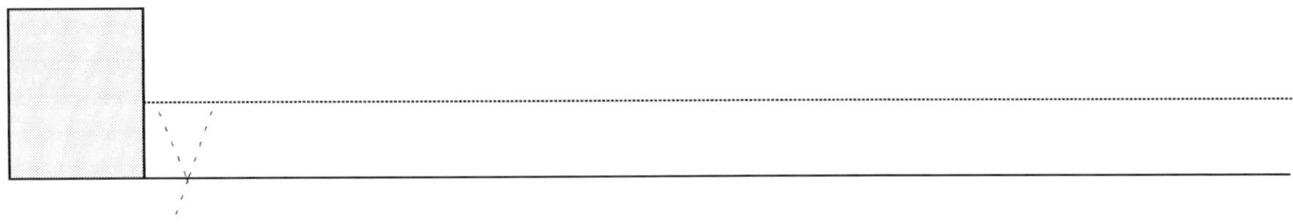

Day 82

Name and Address

Write your name and address as best as you can.

Day 83

Zero

Write the word zero. Then trace the zero and write a full row of them.

0

Day 84

One

Write the word one. Then trace the one and write a full row of them.

Day 85

Two

Write the word two. Then trace the two and write a full row of them.

2

Day 86

Three

Write the word three. Then trace the three and write a full row of them.

3

Day 87

Four

Write the word four. Then trace the four and write a full row of them.

4

Day 88

Five

Write the word five. Then trace the five and write a full row of them.

5

Day 89

Six

Write the word six. Then trace the six and write a full row of them.

6

Day 90

Seven

Write the word seven. Then trace the seven and write a full row of them.

7

Day 91

Eight

Write the word eight. Then trace the eight and write a full row of them.

8

Day 92

Nine

Write the word nine. Then trace the nine and write a full row of them.

9

Day 93

Ten

Write the word ten. Trace the ten. Then put your finger down next to it. On the other side of your finger write the next ten. Leave a finger width's space between each ten. Write a full row of them.

10

Day 94

Eleven

Write the word eleven. Trace eleven and write a full row. Leave a finger width's space between each eleven.

Day 95

Twelve

Write the word twelve. Then trace the twelve and write a full row of them. Don't forget to leave a space between each one you write.

12

Day 96

Thirteen

Write the word thirteen. Then trace the thirteen and write a full row of them. Don't forget to leave a space between each one you write.

13

Day 97

Fourteen

Write the word fourteen. Then trace the fourteen and write a full row of them.

14

Day 98

Fifteen

Write the word fifteen. Then trace the fifteen and write a full row of them.

15

Day 99

Sixteen

Write the word sixteen. Then trace the sixteen and write a full row of them.

16

Day 100

Seventeen

Write the word seventeen. Then trace the number and write a full row of them.

17

Day 101

Eighteen

Write the word eighteen. Then trace the eighteen and write a full row of them.

18

Day 102

Nineteen

Write the word nineteen. Then trace the nineteen and write a full row of them.

19

Day 103

Twenty

Write the word twenty. Then trace the twenty and write a full row of them.

20

Day 104

Writing Words

Write these words: lunch, pitch, match, rich, such.

Day 105

Writing Words

Write these words: bath, pack, will, munch, dash.

Day 106

Writing Words

Write these words: ring, thing, king, sang, bang.

Day 107

Writing Words

Write these words: rung, song, hung, long, sang.

Day 108

Writing Words

Write these words: catching, jumping, sending, hanging.

Day 109

Writing Words

Write these sentences: The bank is pink. The rink is red.

Day 110

Writing Words

Write these words: sunk, hunk, wink, thank, sinking.

Day 111

Writing Words

Write these pairs of words on each line. Put your finger down to make a space between the words.

mad made - tap tape - can cane - back bake

Day 112

Writing Words

Write these pairs of words on each line. Put your finger down to make a space between the words.

bit bite - hid hide - fill file - lick like

Day 113

Writing Words

Write these pairs of words on each line. Put your finger down to make a space between the words.

hop hope - not note - lone home - jock joke

Day 114

Writing Words

Write these pairs of words on each line. Put your finger down to make a space between the words.

cub cube - us use - cut cute - duck duke

Day 115

Writing Sentences

Write this sentence. You will have to use more than one line. Make sure to leave a space between words. Also make sure the first letter is a capital, big letter I and ends with a period. Then read your sentence.

In the heat I feel weak each week.

Day 116

Writing Sentences

Write this sentence. You will have to use more than one line. Make sure to leave a space between words. Also make sure the first letter is a capital, a big letter, and that the sentence ends with a period. Then read your sentence.

He is teaching pitching.

Day 117

Writing Sentences

Write this sentence. You will have to use more than one line. Make sure to leave a space between words. Also make sure the first letter is a capital, a big letter, and that the sentence ends with a period. Then read your sentence.

Take hold of his hand.

Day 118

Writing Sentences

Write this sentence. You will have to use more than one line. Make sure to leave a space between words. Also make sure the first letter is a capital, big letter, and that it ends with a question mark. Then read your sentence.

Can he find me here in this shop?

Day 119

Writing Sentences

Write this sentence. You will have to use more than one line. Make sure to leave a space between words. Also make sure the first letter is a capital and that you end with a period. Then read your sentence.

His big kite will win the game.

<u>Day 120</u>

Writing Words

Write these words: getting, popping, fitting, helping, telling. Then read your words.

Day 121

Writing Words

Write these words: hummed, jumped, melted, fanned, mapped. Then read your words.

Day 122

Writing Words

Write these words: tanner, kicker, bagger, jumper, helper. Then read your words.

Day 123

Writing Words

Write these words: reader, rider, leading, raking, voted, leaped. Then read your words.

Day 124

Writing Words

Write these words: back, backing, backed, bake, baking, baked. Then read your words.

Day 125

Writing Words

Write these words: itself, cannot, bedtime, sunset, forget. Then read your words.

Day 126

Writing Words

Write these words: bikes, dogs, rocks, wishes, lunches, pitches. Then read your words.

Day 127

Writing Sentences

Write this sentence. You will have to use more than one line. Make sure to leave a space between words. Also make sure the first letter is a capital and that you end with a period. Then read your words.

We expect him to fix his box.

Day 128

Writing Words

Write these words: she, shellfish, shelves, Sherry, shopping, shut. Then read your words.

Day 129

Writing Sentences

Write this sentence. You will have to use more than one line. Make sure to leave a space between words. Also make sure the first letter is a capital and that you end with a period. Then read your sentence.

I am washing my ship.

Day 130

Writing Words

Write these words: cheap, checkers, chips, chapped, chattering, chased. Then read your words.

Day 131

Writing Sentences

Write this sentence. You will have to use more than one line. Make sure to leave a space between words. Also make sure the first letter is a capital and that you end with a period. Then read your sentence.

The teacher checked the tests.

Day 132

Writing Sentences

Write this sentence. Make sure to leave a space between words. Also make sure the first letter is a capital and that you end with a question mark. Then read your sentence.

Why is the weather so cold?

Day 133

Writing Sentences

Write this sentence. Make sure to leave a space between words. Also make sure the first letter is a capital and that you end with a period. Then read your sentence.

There is the thin path that leads home.

Day 134

Writing Sentences

Write this sentence. Make sure to leave a space between words. Also make sure the first letter is a capital and that you end with a period. Then read your sentence.

We think we hear a duck quacking.

Day 135

Writing Sentences

Write this sentence. Make sure to leave a space between words. Also make sure the first letter is a capital and that you end with a question mark. Then read your sentence.

Where is she chasing him so quickly?

Day 136

Writing Words

Write these words: blooper, clapping, slapped, flip, plates, glad. Then read your words.

Day 137

Writing Words

Write these words: cleaner, sleeping, sleds, clogged, slipper, cleared. Then read your words.

Day 138

Writing Sentences

Write these sentences. Make sure to leave a space between words and between the sentences. Also make sure the first letter of each is a capital and that you end each with a period. Then read your sentences.

I am sleepy. Please be quiet so I can go to sleep.

Day 139

Writing Sentences

Write this sentence. Make sure to leave a space between words. Also make sure the first letter is a capital and that you end with a period. Then read your sentence.

She got a smear on her smock.

Day 140

Writing Words

Write these words: stepped, still, spitting, sticks, stopped, speedy. Then read them.

Day 141

Writing Words

Write these words: skill, sketched, skipping, scared, scales, scab. Then read your words.

<u>Day 142</u>

Writing Words

Write these words: still, spotting, stunned, snaps, smash, smelly. Then read your words.

Day 143

Calendar

Fill in the name of the month. Find where 1 belongs and then fill in the day numbers in each day's box.

____

Sunday	Monday	Tuesday	Wednesday	Thursday	Friday	Saturday

Day 144

Writing Words

Write these words: Fred, brick, props, cracked, dragging, gripped. Then read your words.

Day 145

Writing Sentences

Write this sentence. Make sure to leave a space between words. Also make sure the first letter is a capital and that you end with a period. Then read your sentence.

He has a trick up his sleeves.

Day 146

Writing Sentences

Write this sentence. Make sure to leave a space between words. Also make sure the first letter is a capital and that you end with a period. Then read your sentence.

Glitter is fun to put on crafts.

Write: 1, 2, 3, 4, 5

Day 147

Writing Words

Write these word pairs on the lines: arm - farm, ark – bark, art – part, car - card. Then read your words.

Write: 6, 7, 8, 9, 10

<u>Day 148</u>

Writing Words

Write these word pairs on the lines: for - Ford, or – horn, war – warm, fork - fort. Then read your words.

Write: 11, 12, 13, 14, 15

Day 149

Writing Sentences

Write this sentence. Make sure to leave a space between words. Also make sure the first letter is a capital and that you end with a period. Then read your sentence.

Four stores get awards for selling floor boards.

Write: 16, 17, 18, 19, 20

Day 150

Writing Sentences

Write this sentence. Make sure to leave a space between words. Also make sure the first letter is a capital and that you end with a period. Then read your sentence.

The girl got hurt falling in the dirt.

Write: 21, 22, 23, 24, 25

Day 151

Writing Sentences

Write this sentence. Make sure to leave a space between words. Also make sure the first letter is a capital and that you end with a period. Then read your sentence.

The early bird gets the worm.

Write: 26, 27, 28, 29, 30

Day 152

Writing Words

Write these word pairs on the lines: sail - tail, rain – main, hair – fair, maid - paid. Then read your words. Make sure to leave a space between the words!

Write: 31, 32, 33, 34, 35

Day 153

Writing Words

Write these word pairs on the lines: say - way, play – clay, gray – pray, day - today. Then read your words. Make sure to leave a space between the words!

Write: 36, 37, 38, 39, 40

Day 154

Writing Words

Write these word pairs on the lines: coat - boat, toe – goes, low – below, oat – float. Then read your words. Make sure to leave a space between the words!

Write: 41, 42, 43, 44, 45

Day 155

Writing Sentences

Write this sentence. Make sure to leave a space between words. Also make sure the first letter is a capital and that you end with a period. Then read your sentence.

The wind blows softly and the stream flows slowly.

Write: 46, 47, 48, 49, 50

Day 156

Writing Words

Write this sentence. Make sure to leave a space between words. Also make sure the first letter is a capital and that you end with a period. Then read your sentence.

Eat your fruit stew with a spoon.

Write: 51, 52, 53, 54, 55

Day 157

Writing Words

Write these words on the lines: believe, field, parties, thief, puppies. Then read your words. Make sure to leave a space between the words!

Write: 56, 57, 58, 59, 60

Day 158

Writing Words

Write these word pairs on the lines: lie - tie, fly – flies, spy – spies, try – tries. Then read your words. Make sure to leave a space between the words!

Write: 61, 62, 63, 64, 65

Day 159

Writing Words

Write these words on the lines: light, type, goodbye, buying, my - by. Then read your words. Make sure to leave a space between the words!

Write: 66, 67, 68, 69, 70

Day 160

Writing Words

Write this sentence. Make sure to leave a space between words. Also make sure the first letter is a capital and that you end with a period. Then read your sentence.

The boat will be waiting in the harbor tonight.

Write: 71, 72, 73, 74, 75

Day 161

Writing Words

Write this sentence. Make sure to leave a space between words. Also make sure the first letter is a capital and that you end with a period. Then read your sentence.

Use that spice twice to make the rice.

Write: 76, 77, 78, 79, 80

Day 162

Writing Words

Write this sentence. Make sure to leave a space between words. Also make sure the first letter is a capital and that you end with a question mark. Then read your sentence.

Do you see what's in the center circle ring at the circus?

Write: 81, 82, 83, 84, 85

Day 163

Writing Words

Write your whole name.

Write: 86, 87, 88, 89, 90

Day 164

Writing Words

Write your address.

Write: 91, 92, 93, 94, 95

Day 165

Writing Words

Write an "I love you" note to someone.

Write: 96, 97, 98, 99, 100

Day 166

Writing Numbers

Write your phone number.

Day 167

Write the name of the story you listened to today.

Count to 100 and fill in the missing numbers.

1	2		4	5	6	7		9	10
11		13	14	15		17	18	19	20
21	22	23		25	26	27	28		30
31	32	33	34	35	36	37	38	39	
41	42	43	44		46	47	48	49	50
	52	53	54	55	56		58	59	60
61	62		64	65	66	67	68	69	70
71		73	74	75		77	78	79	80
81	82		84	85	86	87	88		90
	92	93		95	96	97		99	100

Day 168

Writing

Write about your story.

Day 169

Writing

Write about your story.

Day 170

Writing

Write about your story.

Day 171

Writing

Write about your story.

Day 172

Writing

Write about your story.

Day 173

Writing

Write, "I am __________ years old." Fill in how old you are!

Day 174

Writing

Write about your story.

Day 175

Writing

Write about your story.

Day 176

Writing

Write about your story.

Day 177

Writing

Write about your story.

Day 178

Writing

Write about your story. Write your city or state, and write your country.

Day 179

Writing

Write tale and tail.

Day 180

Writing

Write about your story.

I hope you are enjoying learning with Easy Peasy All-in-One Homeschool.

Easy Peasy offers quality homeschool resources for families around the globe.

EP seeks to free families from the burden of pursuing the "perfect" and encourages them to let it be "enough." Each family and each child is different, and we seek to provide the resources to enable your family to be who you were meant to be.

Made in the USA
Lexington, KY
27 September 2016